W9-BMA-850

"Martin Helldorfer's *Prayer When It's Hard to Pray* is not exactly a book for beginners. With his usual clear insight into the pilgrimage of the human person, he gives us material that will cause us to nod our heads in agreement and to open our mouths in momentary surprise. *Prayer When It's Hard to Pray* is a companion to prayer, allowing us to reflect on the difficulties that must be present when we seek to bring our very selves to this intimacy of encounter with God. For all its stark realism, *Prayer When It's Hard to Pray* is a book filled with hope."

† Daniel L. Ryan
Bishop of Springfield, IL

"This book is about the utter simplicity of prayer that comes to a person who grows still and then knows that God is revealed in every person, event, and life change. It is the expression of a person who has found and crossed the threshold of awareness that mystics point to. Helldorfer encourages the reader that once this threshold of awareness has been crossed, even once, the art of prayer is experienced as the humble and quiet acceptance of the fact that God is revealed in the realities of life. The reader has only to grow still enough to hear and attend to God stirring everywhere."

Sr. Ruth McGoldrick, S.P.
President, Sisters of Providence of Holyoke

"Dr. Helldorfer's words grab you, slow you down, and quiet your mind, body, and heart. His thoughts about prayer evoke a prayerful disposition. As you take up his book, you move from noisy to quiet, from the profane to the sacred, from the exterior to the interior, and from being a tourist to becoming a pilgrim. He thoughtfully helps you to see and hear the world around you as God's stirrings of the moment."

Vincent Bilotta, Ph.D.
President, Formation Consultation Services, Inc.

"Prayer When It's Hard To Pray is a delightfully inspiring reflection on prayer written in a conversational, poetic style. It is marked by simplicity, yet opens the door to a mystery and mysticism with which even the average reader can identify. Helldorfer treats of silence, of the 'desert experience,' of 'God's absence' as an invitation to yet another discovery in the spiritual life, as an indication of growth. His approach to prayer is an integrated one involving mind, body, and spirit, stretching well beyond the formal times of prayer.

"This is one of the most encouraging and refreshing books on prayer in recent years. It is one you will not really be finished with when you have read the last page!"

Rosemary Laliberte, R.S.M.
President, Sisters of Mercy
Regional Community of Providence

"Prayer When It's Hard to Pray strikes just the right note. Those already at ease with prayer will recognize with a smile the truths they have already discovered. Those who are hearing in a new way God's invitation to prayer will find solid, encouraging, and trustworthy guidance in these pages.

"The format, language, and style of this book are profoundly—and deceptively—simple. It distills into one volume wisdom that could fill many. Open to any page and be touched by a challenging insight, a confirmation, a question, a reassurance. Contem-porary believers sometimes claim to have neither the time to pray nor the time to learn about it. Dr. Helldorfer has effectively challenged that claim."

Gertrude Foley, S.C., D.Min.
Major Superior, Sisters of Charity of Seton Hill

PRAYER

When It's Hard to Pray

MARTIN HELLDORFER

TWENTY-THIRD PUBLICATIONS

Mystic, CT 06355

Acknowledgments

I gratefully acknowledge my indebtedness to those who knowingly and unknowingly shaped this book: Sr. Marie Kraus, Dr. Claire Brissette, Br. James Leahy, Sr. Rose Clarisse Gadoury, and Dr. Thomas Tyrrell.

Though presumptuous, I add the names of St. John Baptist de la Salle and Thomas Merton.

Most importantly, I thank the former residents and staff of the House of Affirmation as well as the patients and staff at Villa St. John Vianney Hospital. The life that we share is, indeed, a most extraordinary gift.

Revised edition 1994

Twenty-Third Publications
185 Willow Street
P.O. Box 180
Mystic, CT 06355
(203) 536-2611
800-321-0411

ISBN 0-89622-602-6
Library of Congress Catalog Card Number 94-60351
Printed in the U.S.A.

reface

Isn't there a time when all of us find prayer difficult? *Prayer When It's Hard to Pray* was written for those who find it hard, if not impossible, to pray. It is not in itself an exhortation to pray. Neither is it an apologia for prayer. It is simply a reflection on the experience of prayer. In that sense it is a guide.

One person has written the text, but many have authored it. They are the women and men who have shared their life experiences with me in many differing ways. Their lives lie behind these words, although no one person's experience is represented.

A word of caution. This book is a guide, but no solutions to specific problems nor answers to unsettling questions about prayer are given. It is a guide insofar as the experiences of these men and women lie behind the reflections.

Prayer When It's Hard to Pray is a guide in another way: It will leave you with a sense of how you can help yourself in regard to prayer. See if this isn't the case. After you have read the book meditatively and prayerfully over a period of time, hold on to it for a while. If it has helped your prayer in any way, note those reflections that you found particularly helpful, and keep it on your bookshelf for another day when praying may again become difficult, and reading it may again be helpful.

It is my hope that you will find this volume helpful in developing your spirituality.

*D*edication

In memory of John, my father

Contents

PART ONE

Why We Pray

*L*ord,
Open our eyes to see your hand at work
    in the splendor of creation
        and in the beauty of human life.
Touched by your hand our world is holy.
Help us to cherish the gifts
    that surround us,
    to share your blessings
    with our brothers and sisters,
    and to experience the joy of life
        in your presence.

–Prayer,
Seventeenth Sunday
of Ordinary Time

*I*f you pick up a book
   "and simply read it through,
   you are wasting your time.
As soon as any thought
   stimulates your mind or your heart
   put the book down
   because your meditation has begun.
To think that you are somehow obliged
   to follow the author of the book
   to a particular conclusion
   would be a great mistake.
It may happen that the conclusion
   does not apply to you.
God may . . . have planned
   to give you quite a different grace
   than the one the author suggests
   you might be needing."

                              –Thomas Merton
                              New Seeds of Contemplation

*T*hen Jesus went with them
to a place called Gethsemane,
and he said to his disciples,
"Sit here,
while I go over there and pray."
And taking with him
Peter and the two sons of Zebedee,
he began to be sorrowful
and troubled.
Then he said to them,
"My soul is very sorrowful,
even to death;
remain here, and watch with me."
And going a little farther
he fell on his face and prayed.

–Matthew 26:36–39

*P*rayer is a movement toward intimacy.
It cannot be forced.
Time is needed for it to develop
    and its price is costly.
A lifetime of shared joys and sorrows
    is involved.
To force prayer is as ineffective
    as efforts to force intimacy.
Prayer, like intimacy,
    is an almost unrecognizable
        and wordless realization
        of what has come to be.

*P*hrased another way,
    prayer is the posture of someone
    who at all times and in every place
    knows that everything is from God.

Prayer is also a word we use
    to describe a relationship.
It is a word to speak of the bond
    between God and ourselves.
It is a bond
    likened to the love
    between mother and child—
    unbreakable,
    but hardly untroubled.

*T*he language of prayer
   is that of love.
To ask how to pray
   is like asking how to love.
We start with words but end in silence.

When we grow in love,
   especially romantic love,
   we want to voice that love
      time and again.
But words are not enough.
Silence is needed.
A man grew to love a woman.
Without being aware of his nervousness,
   he frequently assured her of his love.
One day he noticed a pleading in her eyes.
"Hold me," she said,
   and from that moment he knew that
   there is a time to be wordless.
Why solitary prayer?
Because there is a time for it.

*T*he silence of love is a place of rest.
Think of prayer as such a place.

God has spoken to us
   in the person of Jesus.
He was remarkably silent
   in the midst of his life.
We are God's continued revelation.
Our lives are a prayer.
They are a way of voicing something that
   our lips cannot utter.
We try to find words
   but must be content with silence.
The more we sense the sacredness of
   what we are about,
   the quieter we become.
The prayerful person is silent yet worldly.

*W*hen lives are shared
there is a time for words.
But to reduce a relationship
to words is a mistake.
To reduce prayer to words
is equally unfortunate.

Much of life is lived in silence;
all of life evokes it.

In *The World of Silence*, Max Picard writes,
"When language ceases, silence begins.
But it does not begin
because language ceases.
The absence of language simply makes the
presence of Silence more apparent."

Prayer involves learning to rest.

*A*gain, think of prayer
  as a word we use
  to describe our relationship with God.
We are always in relationship;
  we are always praying.
Quietness is needed to recognize prayer.

We can walk a dozen times
  along a familiar path
  and never notice its beauty.
Stop for a moment; sit down and rest;
  look closely. The world breaks open.
We see what was unseen.
The more contemplative we become,
  the more we notice.
These are the moments
  when we have a hint
  of the Life behind our life.
But the world seldom opens
  without a moment of rest.
Once it yields,
  memory of those moments lingers.

*W*e, too, are God's creation,
   God's work of art.
Often we live as if we are our own.
Failing to make ourselves
   into the persons we are not,
   we become painfully aware of the gap
   between what we want to become
   and what we are.
No wonder we are restless.

The fact is that we are God's work of art,
   wholly and uniquely so.
Suppose we awakened to that truth?
Then our stance toward ourselves
   would be altered in a remarkable way.
If the person beside us
   is also God's work of art,
   what a difference that would make.
We need to quietly accept the fact
   that we are formed preciously.
That truth transforms.

*W*e have to help one another
  find moments of rest.
Sometimes we fear quiet
  because we fear boredom.
We turn on a stereo
  for background music.
We assure ourselves
  that it does not interfere
  with our concentration.
Sometimes we say that after a time
  we hardly hear the radio.

When something that is present
  is not heard
  we are saying that the uttered word no
  longer touches us.
We might say, perhaps too harshly,
  that we have become impervious
  to what has broken into the world.
We have deadened ourselves
  to the extent that the word
  no longer matters.

$\mathscr{W}$e deaden our lives
 when we forget
 that they are rooted in silence.
Silence is the place from which to hear.
If we do not hear,
 we cannot respond.

Think of what would happen
 to our speech
 if there were no pauses
 between our words.
It would become senseless.
Communication would falter.
Without moments of silence
 our activity loses its value.

*O*utward quiet is difficult to find;
    inward silence is even more elusive.
Many times we live so alienated
    from our own inwardness
    that when we find a moment of silence
    we think of it as prayer.
Once quieted
    we then move apart from prayer
    at the moment when
    we are ready for it.

Silence is the ground
    of human involvement,
    be it work or play.
That is why we need to help one another
    become inwardly quiet.
When quieted we are invited
    to become attentive
    to the beauty and goodness of life.
We will also see its violence and injustice.
Before long, persons of prayer
    are led back to the marketplace
    where their presence is so necessary.

"*There* is more silence
than language in love."

–Max Picard
The World of Silence

"It is...in silence
    that we should seek the native soil
    in which faith can grow....
Between that unheard-of happening,
    the Incarnation, and the human person
    silence interposes itself
    as a kind of buffer....
Thus, in approaching God,
    we approach the silence with which
    God is surrounded."

–Gabriel Marcel
Introduction to the World of Silence

"We put frames of words around silence
    and shells of stone and wood
    around emptiness,
    but it is the silence...
    that finally matters
    and out of which
    the Gospel comes as Word."

–Frederick Buechner
Telling the Truth

PART TWO

*Experiences
of Prayer*

*W*e associate the words
   peace and tranquility
   with prayer.
And rightly so.
Yet for many of us,
   prayer is not a comforting experience;
   it is one of emptiness.
Like the poet,
   we feel that there is no face
   on which our gaze can rest;
   there is only endless desert.
When we feel this way,
   nothing is wrong.
The climate of prayer is often,
   if not usually,
   the desert.

*D*eserts are not distant places.
They are within cities
    and as close as our hearts.
They are places of space
    created by absence.
When loved ones move away,
    the desert is terrible.
Consider friendship or marriage.
When two persons pledge their love
    they feel as if they know one another.
However, when they begin to change,
    especially when one changes
    at a pace different from the other,
    the relationship is troubled.
The moment they recognize
    that what has been cannot be recovered
    and that a new relationship
    must be found between them,
    they begin to awaken to the realization
    that they have promised fidelity,
    not constancy.
However, before that discovery is made;
    the two must live
    in a moment of suspension
    when they feel as if
    they have lost each other.
That is a desert.

Something similar happens in prayer.
When we change,
  our relationship to God changes.
We seemingly withdraw
  from one another.
Since we are always changing,
God is always being lost.

We begin therapy.
If successful, that is, if we change,
God will surely be lost.
Our employment affects
  what we see and value.
Change it, and our prayer is affected.
Schooling does the same.
So does romantic love.
Every life experience
  touches our relationship to God.

*H*aven't we lost God before?
Look back over life.

A child of seven
    prays beside his bed for his parents.
His trust is appealing
    and his simplicity disarming.

A youngster of twelve has her God
    beside her as companion and helper.
We smile.

As an adolescent,
    that same person may reject
    the God of his or her younger years.
God is absent.

That same person may find God
    as a young adult.

And so it goes.

*E*ach change creates a gap.
When we look backward in time
    it is relatively easy to admit to the way
    that God is lost and found.
It is more difficult to acknowledge
    the same changes in our own adult life.
However, no one escapes such moments.

"To arrive where you are,
    to get from where you are not,
    you must go by a way
    wherein there is not ecstasy.

In order to arrive
    at what you do not know
    you must go by a way
    which is the way of ignorance.

In order to possess
    what you do not possess
    you must go by the way
    of dispossession.

In order to arrive at what you are not
    you must go through the way
    in which you are not."

                              –T.S. Eliot
                              Four Quartets

*F*or some,
   the gap is extended.
When this occurs we live in a desert.
That is unsettling.

For others,
   the moment of suspension is an instant.
Change is not troubling for them.
The new intermingles with the old
   in a way that smooths transitions.

If life experience is drawn as a line,
   a few could depict their lives
   as relatively continuous.
They are the persons for whom change
   is not particularly troubling.
They are molded slowly by everyday life.

*O*thers know desert experiences
   only now and again.
At times there are periods
   when they are settled.
Their life experience is marked by
   stops and starts.

Still others
   know what it is
   to have one major life crisis
   that seems to divide their lives
   into halves.
They speak of a before and after
   of one never-to-be-forgotten
   troubling time.

*A*nd some know the feeling
  of living in a near-continuous desert
  where tranquil moments are as rare
  as the moments of crisis are for others.
They live within gaps.

When in crisis,
  when something or someone is lost,
  there is seldom an awareness
  and certainly no assurance
  that the moment will pass.
We are suspended.
That is what is so unsettling.
It feels as if there is no end.
Some paths may be easier;
  no one way is better.

"There is a waiting
which is desire.

There is a silence
full of sound.

There is a patience,
wide as a world aburst with strength....

There is a waiting which is a growing,
a waiting with the swell
and fall of breathing.

"*There* is a waiting like a wake,
the flicker of a solitary star
the only light,
the candle,
a wavering sign, an uncertain token....

There is a waiting
    chilling my bones....

There is a waiting loud like a universe
    far gone in gestation.

There is a loneliness tight with terror,
    ready to break adrift,
        to roam the dark alluring sea."

–Jacques Theuws
Transcendental Meditations

$\mathcal{B}$ut standing by the cross of Jesus
   were his mother,
   and his mother's sister,
Mary the wife of Clopas,
   and Mary Magdalene.

                              –John 19:25

The desert is a time when words falter.
The Eucharist is called
   the sacrament of the Real Presence.
We need a theology of the Real Absence.

*G*od's absence is a gift,
however unwelcome.
It is a hint of change,
   an indication of growth,
   and a path toward depth.
There is no movement without crisis
   nor depth without loss.
Nevertheless we often think
   that something is wrong
   when we feel as we do.
We say to ourselves:
   what good is suffering?
Of what value is emptiness?

Augustine wrote
   that Jesus departed
   from the sight of his followers
   so that they might find
   him in their hearts.
The absence of God is the invitation
   to another discovery,
   not only in our hearts
   but in our involvement as well.

*T*o glimpse the value of suffering,
   recall those to whom
   we turn when in need.
Do we look for those
   who have been protected
   from suffering?
On the contrary,
   we search for persons
   who have known it.
If there is a crisis today,
   it is that we protect
   one another from change.
The cost is depth.
What home, rectory, or community
   creates a space
   for those who struggle with disbelief?

*W*hen is there time for emptiness
  in our lives?
Yet without such crisis moments
  there is no depth.
No, there is little need to worry
  when we struggle with prayer.
The time for concern
  is when we are pious.
Remember: Love is faithful,
  not necessarily constant.

PART THREE

*Impediments
to Prayer*

*C*an we help ourselves
   when unable to pray?
Yes.
We can stop praying.
Better still,
   we can stop trying to pray.

When one way of praying has died,
   why repeat that way so doggedly?
Why not move in another direction?
If a door is locked,
   why not try a window?
If we seem trapped,
   why not sit for a moment
   and look about?
What have we to lose?

*O*ne of the problems with prayer
is that it is sometimes a relationship
that we construct.
Without knowing it,
we build a prayer life
that serves any number of functions,
often protective ones.
To let go of that approach is threatening.
Yet, if God is truly lost,
certainly our decision to stop praying
cannot make things worse.
It is not prayer
that we find difficult to relinquish;
it is our need to control.

*R*ecall the Scriptures.
Isn't it God's faithfulness
    on which we rely?
If we let go of prayer,
    will God let go of us?
Hardly.
To think otherwise is to lose perspective.
Our relationship with God rests on love,
    not equality.
In the desert we need trust
    more than effort.
Discipline is for the city,
    surrender for the desert.

Instead of fretting,
    place the Scriptures
    beside an easy chair.
Let them rest there.
Their presence will be a sign of our desire
    as well as our inability to pray.
Some day when we are less restless
    we may turn to them
    in a way that we would turn
    to any cherished words.
But for now let them rest.

*W*e can also learn to wait.

That, too, is difficult.
We will return to prayer sometime
   but when and where that will be
   remains unknown.
There is very little need to be anxious
   about that moment.
We are held by God
   even when we flounder.
Waiting is an act of faith,
   not rebellion.

"Today is the first day of spring.
I've waited for this day
   and have yearned for its warmth.
But it snowed yesterday
   and this first day of spring
   is as wet and cold as any day of winter.
I've been feeling down all day
   and I spent most of the morning
   complaining about the weather.

"There is something humorous
in the way that I live.
I seem to endure the present moment
by anticipating a future one
and when the future arrives
I destroy it by feeling
that it is other than it should be.
My attitude that the present
is not-as-it-should-be
robs the moment
of some of its simplest joys
and sorrows.
This may be one of the reasons
why I have such a difficult time
trying to pray.
After figuring out what prayer should be,
I then end up berating myself
that it is not as it should be
or else I try to muster the will power
to make it the way it ought to be.
What a funny person I am.
I think that I need
a lot more snowy days in spring."

–Anonymous

All of us do.

*I*n the moment of waiting,
   listen:
   New life stirs.

To discover that life is not easy.
Stern inward voices
   may keep us from relaxing.
"Hurry," they say,
   "do something.
Try harder.
You are on dangerous ground.
Something is wrong.
Strengthen your back,
   tighten your muscles,
   awaken your will,
   and join your hands."
Many people do.

There is no need for that kind of violence.
Stern voices need to be acknowledged,
   not followed.
What we do need is sensitivity
   to less strident voices
   from quieter places.

*G*rowth cannot be rushed.
Timing is involved.
A wisdom saying advises us
   to wait with open hands
   beneath ripening fruit.
The wise person will know
   the moment to reach.
It will correspond to the moment
   that the fruit falls.
That is what waiting is all about.
It is knowing the moment of readiness.

It is not what we believe about God
   that is so important;
   it is what God knows of us
   that is so valuable.

*W*e can do something else
　　when unable to pray.
We can let go of our preoccupation
　　with what has died
　　and look in the direction
　　of what is living.
Follow that path.

When we focus on what is lively,
　　we open ourselves
　　to discover the prayer
　　that is already present but unseen.
Discipline, fasting, vigils,
　　and the seemingly dark places
　　of asceticism
　　are valuable
　　but they are not the only way to God.
In fact, they are often distorted ones.
Everyday life with its pleasures and pain,
　　beauty and ugliness,
　　is rich soil for prayer.
Look for God in its shadows.

*W*e live in one world,
   known to be two.
The same reality that is profane
   at one moment
   is sacred at another.
This world and another world,
   the profane and the sacred,
   are neither opposites nor identical.
Moments of explicit prayer are times
   when the two worlds merge.
That is why prayer is silent;
   we are held in two worlds
   where there is no possibility of speech
   only a self-forgetful, wordless, resting
Presence.

*I*nstead of saying prayers,
   be still long enough
   to hear the quieting note
   of God's silent presence.

We can help ourselves
   inestimably each day
   by going in search
   of something beautiful.
When found,
   do not take it home;
   let it stay where found.
At first we may notice roses.
Soon we will find beautiful things
   in the most unlikely places.

*A*nd lastly,
   pray by doing.

When unable to pray,
   let everything,
   work included,
   be a prayer.
Forget about holy words
   and pious feelings.
Become worldly.
Invest in the work at hand.
Is it a job?
Work well.
It is a conversation?
Be attentive.
Is it a book?
Enjoy it.
A meal?
Relish it.
This is not pretense;
   it is another act of faith.

*T*here is a time
   when a kiss expresses love.
To imagine that a kiss
   is the only way to show love
   is unfortunate.
The moment of prayer is a particular way
   to express love.
It is not the only way.
We can love God
   and never know a moment
   of untroubled prayer.
A relationship of love
   is not formed by a momentary act
   but in the life that surrounds it.
In every relationship
   we have to look for ways
   to express love.
No single act is privileged.
When unable to pray
   with words and sentiment,
   move toward the world
   of involvement.

*A*gain stern voices will be heard.
"Don't you know the error involved
   in believing that work is prayer?"
"Haven't you ever heard of the parent
   who shows love by doing only?
Isn't that enough to warn you
   against making work into prayer?"

Those thoughts are a warning
   but not a deterrent.
There is a sacredness in the workplace.
Activity expresses love.
Doing may not be everything
   when we are speaking of love,
   but it is something.

PART FOUR

Times for Prayer

*S*omeday, sometime,
   there may come a moment
   when we are inclined
   to pray in a formal way.
That desire is a gift.
No, it is not an invitation
   to an unusual
   nor to a more intimate
   relationship with God.
Rather, it is an invitation
   to become aware of a relationship
   of love that is already present.
Everyday awareness is sleepy.
When we move into a moment of prayer,
   it is as if the threshold that separates
   the known from the unknown
   is lowered.
We awake for a time.

There is no need
   to take formal time for prayer.
No one will suffer if we do not.
No one will be punished.

*E*fforts to pray that rise from guilt
   reflect good will
   but they are not
   the fertile soil for intimacy.
Again, someday, sometime,
   there may come a moment when we are
   inclined to pray.
When that moment comes,
   we are well advised to listen.

Here, too,
   we need gentleness toward ourselves.
If we do not listen
   we need not fear the consequences.
There are those who say
   that if we do not respond
   to the invitation when given,
   it will be withdrawn.
Do not believe them.
If something is about to
   come into awareness,
   it is not easy to stop its emergence.
Love is faithful
as well as haunting.

*W*hen the moment to pray comes
we will know what to do.
Prayer is an art of sorts,
a moment of self-forgetfulness
when every stirring within the soul
is drawn before God.

Some will say
responding to the moment is easy:
All that is required
is to lift one's mind and heart to God.
It is true that such a gesture
is all that is needed
but it is far from easy.

*S*urrender is involved.
Ask anyone who has shed a shell of piety,
   rebellion,
     or disbelief
     if you want to know how difficult it is
     to surrender.
When all we have known is the desert,
   we develop protective shells.
To pray involves such simplicity
   that most of us stand wary.
However, once the shells are worn thin
   or even break
   —if only for an instant—
   we are inevitably pulled
   to find time for prayer.
Memory of a glimpse is all that is needed.

*S*ome will find time for prayer
  in the morning.
A kiss upon waking
  is expressive of a whole way
  of living in relationship.
Words at such a time are unnecessary
  and can even clutter the sentiment
  that is expressed.
An extended and profound
  bow before God
  upon waking
  is an unfathomably rich prayer.
Because we are remembering persons,
  the kiss and the bow
  linger throughout the day.
Perhaps that is why
  there is morning prayer.

We move into prayer
  when the God
  about whom we are thinking
  becomes the person
  with whom we are present.

*S*ome will find time for prayer
   in the evening.
At nightfall we have the day behind
   and the night before us.
Prayer at that time is as different
   from prayer in the morning
   as sentiments at sunset
   differ from those at sunrise.
There is no need to praise
   one time over the other.
The heart knows a time for both.

*P*rayer involves not only
   the mind and heart,
   but the body as well.
We are wholly bodily persons;
   not only, but wholly so.
Look at a discus thrower
   poised and ready to throw.
A glance is enough to know
   what he is about.
If a woman is bent over a desk
   with a book in front of her
   we surmise that she is studying.
Such persons can deceive us.
The discus thrower could be searching
   the ground for something lost
   and the woman at her desk
   might be sleeping.
The possibility of deceiving ourselves
   or others is not the point.
The fact is that our bodily presence
   speaks to what we are about.
If we want to throw a discus
   we have to look like discus throwers.
Human action, including prayer,
   entails expressing ourselves
   in bodily ways
   that reflect what we are about.

*B*ecoming expressive is not easy.
Again, it is a question of surrender.
As soon as we express ourselves
we are exposed.
We are forced, as it were,
    from our inwardness.
Once exposed, commitment follows.
Lovers know this.
What lovers want to stay in their minds?
When love is reduced to mindfulness
    it soon ends.
The challenge is to live in such a way
    that the inward and outward
    harmonize.
No wonder we are inclined
    to make prayer into an inward affair.
That grants freedom,
    or at least the look of freedom.
It also breeds isolation.

*W*hen inclined to pray
    we need to remember to lift our arms,
    bow our heads, drop to our knees,
    or find some way to manifest
    what stirs within.
This is just as hard to do as to surrender
    to the fact that we are loved.
Sometimes it takes years.

For every minute of prayer,
spend two reflecting on life
apart from prayer.

*A*wareness of ourselves
as bodily persons
may help us avoid
some of the distortions that rise
when we try to develop a prayer life.
For instance, centuries of talk
about prayer
have made it into an esoteric activity.
There are rules galore
about what we should or should not do
with our bodies.
There is talk of how to breathe, eat,
and control the senses.
Some tell us of the necessity
to relax each part
of our bodies progressively.
Others advise us of the need
to empty our minds.
As helpful as these suggestions
are at times, they often enough
mold us into religious artifacts
rather than loving persons.

*W*hen with a loved one,
   do we try to empty
   ourselves of all thoughts?
Do we need to control our attention
   when we embrace someone?
Hardly.
The more we are expressive,
   the more we recognize
   that we are wholly bodily persons.
As this awareness awakens,
   the need to control ourselves
   is lessened.
If we let ourselves become
   expressive during prayer,
   prayer becomes easier.

*M*ost importantly,
   formal prayer has a rhythm all its own.
Managers have schedules;
   lovers do not.
The pattern of prayer changes
   from day to day and year to year.
There is no guarantee
   that our rhythm will be daily.
Maybe it is weekly
   with Saturdays and Sundays
   as times of formal prayer.
Maybe it is yearly
   when the summer brings its gifts.
Some look back on their lives
   and recognize the rhythm
   in terms of years.
No one pattern is better than another.
The challenge is to respect
   the changing rhythms of our own lives.
That involves remaining quiet enough
   to hear God's stirrings at any moment.
When we try to mold ourselves
   into persons we are not,
   we may develop the look of virtue
   but we will have to live
   with the consequences
   of being unfaithful to ourselves.

*A*nd lastly,
   when the moment to pray comes,
   pray in that place.
There is no need to find a special one.
All places are sacred.
Each house and room,
   every forest and city is holy.
Some places, such as churches
   or the ground where
   a loved one is buried,
   are especially sacred.
Even so, there is no need
   to choose those places to pray.
We are in a sacred place
   when the moment comes.

Prayer is no guarantee
   that we will feel peaceful.
When we pray God's light shines upon us.
That light can leave us agitated
   as well as peaceful.

*I*f prayer leads us toward
   increased flexibility,
   openness,
   and responsibility,
   we have a hint that our efforts
   to pray are informed.
If we find ourselves increasingly isolated
   from others,
   we have a hint
that our efforts are misdirected.

Prayer has to do with a way of living.
It is not one activity
   beside so many others.

*O*ften we fail to take time to pray
because we have the haunting fear
that something will be asked of us
if we pray.
That fear is well founded.

To stand wordlessly,
quietly,
and at times darkly before God
day after day
changes the way we touch the world
as well as others.

We need to remember that this world is
God's.
Pope John XXIII thought of it as a garden
rather than a museum.
Most of us think of it as raw material.
What a change takes place
when we start to realize
that our home is God's home.

PART FIVE

Entering Into Prayer

*I*n bygone years,
   knights of the Round Table
   left on horseback
   to travel through dark forests
   in search of the Holy Cup.
Each had to find his own path.
That story is everyone's story before God.
Today the horses,
   goblets, and kings
   are gone
   but the forest remains.
The way is still pathless.

*A*re there guides?
Certainly, but be cautious.
The Masters urge us to pose a question
   to the guides we consider.
Ask them what to do
   to keep unholy thoughts
   from disturbing us.
If advised,
   you will know that the guide belongs
   to those who are of no account.

God speaks through every person,
   each happening,
   and all things.
Yet no one speaks for God;
   neither Church, State, neighbor,
nor loved one.
We are always and everywhere
   alone before God.
Sometimes it seems as if
   our only guide is our restlessness.

*W*e are all wayfarers,
   persons journeying on roads
   never before taken.
Another can help us to pray
   by journeying with us.
However, alone or with another,
   the road remains unfamiliar.
Beware of the person who speaks of
   knowing the path.
Beware, too,
   of those who say
   that there are no guides
   and that we are always and everywhere
   isolated from one another.

*B*eing alone is not the same
   as being isolated.
Travel with others.
Trust those who are content
   to share the journey,
   yet do not expect them
   to take an identical path.
The journey is solitary.
All ways of prayer,
   even proven ones,
   are mistaken
   insofar as they are not our own.

*H*ere are three things to remember:

1. God is both hidden
   and manifest,
   distant and near.
None of us knows God;
   all of us do.

2. A person of prayer
   is someone who discovers
   time and again
   what the Hebrews of old knew so well:
   that we unknowingly create idols.
An idol is something that is *instead of*.

3. God hides in pseudonyms.
Our efforts to pray falter
   if for no other reason
   than the god for whom we search
   is not God.
If we desire to pray
   we must live among shadows
   in a world that is sacred
   but that we find commonplace.

*H*ere are two more to remember:

1. Our movement toward God
   is lifelong.
Every balance once achieved
   is cast in doubt
   by changing times and situations.
Our need for conversion is never-ending.
Every decision opens another world
   that entails still another surrender.
Each turning toward God is a partial one.

2. The unsettling reality of prayer
   is that in either ecstasy or depression
   there is never the surety
   that it is God who is there.
Therein lies the incomprehensible
   significance of faith.

*F*inally, two more:

1. Any conception of God
   is inadequate.
Any understanding of prayer is limited.
To say we know God
   or that we have experienced God
   is to walk on dangerous ground.
The young speak that way.
At the same time
   it is foolhardy to say
   that we do not know God
   or that we have never experienced God.
Wisdom has a quietness about it.

2. To be faced by the inescapable,
   metallically cold
   and biting truth
   of our near constant self-seeking
   is to be cleansed by a fire
   that promises, at least as a hope,
   that at some moment we will be silent
   and let God work and speak.

$\mathcal{T}$houghts about prayer
 can leave us
 feeling lonely and frightened.
However, remember
 that the person beside us
 likely feels the same way.
If we realize that, we will feel less fearful
 and more connected to others.
Reach out to them in caring
 and understanding ways.

Of Related Interest...

A New Look at Prayer
Searching for Bliss
William Huebsch
Readers will find a guide for listening to God, for discerning and discovering who they are and who they can be.
ISBN: 0-89622-458-9, 136 pp, $7.95

In God's Presence
Centering Experiences for Circles and Solitudes
William Cleary
Cleary offers psalms, meditations, prayers, and poems that will help both solitary readers and groups find a connection with God.
ISBN: 0-89622-608-5, 144 pp, $9.95

Who We Are Is How We Pray
Charles Keating
This book draws on the 16 personality types identified in the Meyers-Briggs personality profile to find a suitable form and style of spirituality.
ISBN: 0-89622-321-3, 168 pp, $7.95

Available at religious bookstores or from
TWENTY-THIRD PUBLICATIONS
P.O. Box 180 • Mystic, CT 06355
1-800-321-0411